FLYING THE V.O.R.

Airlife Publications

7 St. John's Hill, Shrewsbury, England.

Also by Alan Bramson and Neville Birch
FLIGHT BRIEFING FOR PILOTS, VOLUME 1
FLIGHT BRIEFING FOR PILOTS, VOLUME 2
FLIGHT BRIEFING FOR PILOTS, VOLUME 3
FLIGHT BRIEFING FOR PILOTS, VOLUME 4
A GUIDE TO AIRCRAFT OWNERSHIP
THE TIGER MOTH STORY
FLIGHT EMERGENCY PROCEDURES FOR PILOTS
CAPTAINS AND KINGS
RADIO NAVIGATION FOR PILOTS

Printed in England by Livesey Ltd., Shrewsbury

FLYING THE V.O.R.

by

ALAN BRAMSON

Chairman of the Panel of Examiners and
Liveryman of the Guild of Air Pilots and Air Navigators.

and

NEVILLE BIRCH

Director Hamilton Birch Aviation Ltd., and
Liveryman of the Guild of Air Pilots and Air Navigators.

ILLUSTRATED BY ALAN BRAMSON.

Airlife Publications
England

CONTENTS

PREFACE

Most student pilots work pretty hard at getting a P.P.L. The course embraces navigation, met and air law not to mention the flying syllabus with all those circuits and bumps alongside spins and stalls.

Later in the course the customer is introduced to the charms of cross country flying and while this is supposed to be a map-reading and sweat exercise we know only too well that, although forbidden to do so by his flying instructor, more often than not the rules are bent and use is made of the VOR "to help out a little". At this stage most students have been told little or nothing about this convenient little aid because its use is not part of the P.P.L. course anyway. How therefore do many student pilots learn to use the VOR? The answer is almost invariably through the expert at the bar.

Of course some real experts do indulge in the odd gin and tonic (we are a little partial ourselves as a matter of fact*) but so often the friendly club veteran sitting there drink in hand has never received any real instruction on the subject himself. And if he has there may be a complete lack of ability to explain things clearly, for lucid, unambiguous teaching is, in all walks of life, the exception rather than the rule.

*after the hangar doors are closed.

We have often worried about the amateur pilot, faced as he is with a choice between unqualified instruction at the club bar or the need to study FLIGHT BRIEFING FOR PILOTS, VOL 3, a book we wrote for pilots working towards the full instrument rating. Surely, we thought, there ought to be a little light-hearted book devoted to flying on the VOR, something easy to read and understand. And so here it is, FLYING THE VOR in, to use the well known phrase 'Glorious Technicolour'.

Alan Bramson
Neville Birch

HISTORY

Over the centuries man had turned the problems of flight into a mountain of alarming proportions. When you consider how long he spent just thinking about it while the birds got on with the job one wonders why in this day and age he is so smug and self-congratulatory about his Tridents, BAC111s and Boeings. At one time he even resorted to fabricating stories. Like that lunatic tale of Icarus and his dad flapping their way from a Crete prison on do-it-yourself wings that melted in the sun, and King Bladud, founder of the City of Bath, pioneer aviator who according to Taylor's 'Memorial of English Monarchs (1622)' "—brake his necke becaufe he foar'd too high." Some achievement for a man who never existed!

When a self-satisfied mankind put away the fairy tales and got himself airborne another problem revealed itself, one that exists to this very day. The human animal in the air has an unfortunate habit of getting himself lost. Maps were all very well if you could read them (things looked confusing from aloft) but every so often, in fact more often than not in some parts of the world, nature hit back, a carpet of mist or a blanket of cloud would blot out the land below. Then even the best map readers could only guess. True it was possible to 'inspire' the guess by using a watch, allowing for wind and

1

other discomforts, thus arriving at a **D.R.** (Dead Reckoning) Position. Sometimes, when the fuel ran low and they had to come down through cloud the sums had gone wrong. The term Dead Reckoning then assumed a new significance for the mountain top immersed in cloud has claimed many a press-on aviator.

Very soon a marriage occurred between Flying and that equally new child of technology, Radio. The ability to talk to the ground was, in itself, little more than a source of moral support although the man at the airport could at least advise approaching aircraft that conditions were so bad "even the birds had given up" and so forth. However it was not long before the **Directional** properties of radio were discovered and most of the more important airfields had radio receivers fitted with rotatable aerials complete with compass cards. So when Captain Magdrop was on the way into Croydon in heavy rain with ten fare-paying passengers being violently sick in their wicker chairs, all he had to do was chat up the radio operator on the ground who then twisted his Direction Finding set until the signal faded out. A look at the compass told him that Magdrop and his happy party were, give or take ten degrees or so, 'over there'. Between the wars another radio aid was developed and found widespread use in the USA as well as many other parts of the world. It was called Radio Range, possibly because one of the several things it couldn't do was give you your range from the station. In effect a large transmitter on the ground sent out four signals, two in morse letter 'A' (dot-dash to you) and two in morse letter 'N' (dash-dot). By a process of reflecting the signals into four overlapping quadrants four 'beams' or to use the correct term, 'legs' occurred and while flying in these a pilot would hear both the 'A' and the 'N' signal. Together these two letters in morse can be synchronised to produce a steady note. The legs were arranged to beam down an airway and for many years the system did great service as a radio navigational aid. They even wrote a song about it advising pilots to "—home, home on the range." But it did have these drawbacks. In the first place locating the legs and identifying them could be a long drawn-out business. Then there was the problem of fatigue. This was an audio aid and aircrew used to spend hour after hour listening to dots and dashes, seeking out that steady 'on the beam' signal. It was enough to make you hit the gin at the sight of a dotted line. Then again the aid was only of use to aircraft flying within one of the four legs.

Someone had a vision. How about an aid which radiated an infinite number of bearings, each one capable of being identified on a simple instrument in the aircraft. Radio Range had transmitted in the Medium Frequency band; this new aid would use VHF. Whoever was responsible for giving it a name clearly believed in telling the whole truth and nothing but the truth. He called it:
VERY HIGH FREQUENCY OMNI-DIRECTIONAL RADIO RANGE, or more conveniently, VOR. Today even the smallest of aircraft may be seen fitted with this simple-to-use radio aid which some years ago provoked the claim 'if the Ark had been fitted with VOR, Noah would never have got stuck on Mount Ararat', a reasonable enough assertion but we can all be clever after the event.

HOW DOES IT WORK?

While there is no need for a pilot to have a deep technical understanding of radio aids the basic principles are perhaps of value. It all starts with the radio wave itself, that invisible monster usually depicted as an undulating line which starts at the middle, goes uphill to positive, slides downhill to negative before returning to the middle and starting the **Cycle** all over again (Fig. 1). The number of times per second the wave completes this cycle is called its **Frequency** and a particular part of the cycle is known as the **Phase**. If two transmitters are arranged to send out signals so that the phase of one is, say, at the top of the wave (max. positive) while the other wave is at its lowest point (max. negative) the greatest possible difference in phase will exist between them. We can use a **Phase Comparison** meter to measure this difference and it is this fact, the ability to measure or compare the difference in phase that exists between two radio signals that forms the basis of VOR. If you can visualise that, the moment of truth is near (Fig. 2). The VOR station is usually situated at a reporting point which may or may not be on an airfield. It transmits a fixed or **Reference** signal at a steady phase and this it radiates in all directions. A second signal is arranged to sweep around through 360°, rather like a lighthouse beam. While sweeping, its phase is made to alter so that the relationship between it and the fixed signal is constantly changing throughout all points of the compass.

In the aircraft a VHF Nav. receiver picks up the two signals then feeds them to an instrument situated on the flight panel which is able to measure the difference in phase between the fixed and rotating signals. This is the VOR Meter or **Omnibearing Indicator**. It is so designed that very little skill is

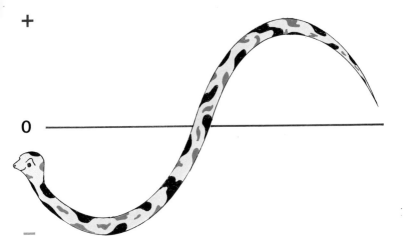

Fig. 1. A radio wave. The snake is displaying one complete cycle.

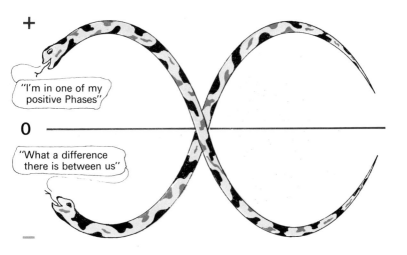

Fig. 2. The basis of VOR, two out-of-phase radio waves.

required to find the magnetic bearing to or from the station and since the fixed and rotating signals vary in relationship according to the aircraft's position around the station, any bearing, or to use the VOR term, **Radial** may be selected for an approach to the transmitter. The radials relate to Magnetic North.

THE OMNI-BEARING INDICATOR

It has long been the writers' belief that if you put a problem to six pilots they will come up with seven answers. So it is with radio manufacturers because, even today, VOR indicators are by no means standard in presentation. However it is possible to talk in general terms and usually the instrument looks like that illustrated in Fig. 3. There is a LEFT/RIGHT or **Deviation Needle** representing magnetic track required. To one side of the instrument case is a knob marked OBS (i.e. Omni-bearing Selector). It is just that. When the knob is turned a compass card rotates against an index thus indicating the radial selected. Sometimes these figures appear at the top of the instrument while other designs have them at the bottom. For convenience the reciprocal is shown in smaller figures at the opposite side of the instrument face. Often there is a small circle in the centre of the dial and four or five dots either side for the purpose of indicating the number of degrees off the selected radial. One or more little windows in the instrument face (according to the design of the equipment) will provide the following information: TO (i.e. TO the VOR beacon) OFF (more about this later) and FROM (which means FROM the VOR beacon). Since the signals that work this masterpiece are inaudible to the human ear it follows that unlike the old Radio Range, pilots are spared

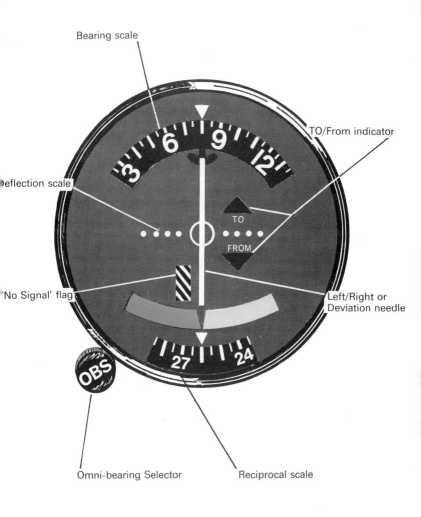

Bearing scale

TO/From indicator

Deflection scale

No Signal' flag

Left/Right or Deviation needle

OBS

Omni-bearing Selector

Reciprocal scale

Fig. 3. Typical VOR indicator. When the instrument is functioning correctly the 'NO SIGNAL' flag disappears and a white arrowhead appears against TO or FROM.

hours and hours of · — and — · so there is no fatigue to the point where one can imagine dots and dashes where none exist at all. This silence does however lend itself to abuse for we are rarely allowed peace in the modern world and VOR beacons are used to broadcast the station call sign in morse which is often accompanied by a non-stop running commentary on airfield weather. Fortunately these can be turned down on the Nav receiver volume control without affecting the operation of the VOR indicator.

USING VOR AS A NAVIGATIONAL AID

Like most other things in life VOR may be used in a number of different ways and the following simple exercise is intended to explain the operation of the equipment in the air. For this purpose imagine you are flying somewhere over Kent, more unsure of your position than usual and already late for a lunch date at Biggin Hill. A glance at the radio chart tells you that a VOR beacon is positioned on the airfield operating on a frequency of 117.5 with the call sign 'BIG' (—··· ·· ——·). To find the QDM (magnetic heading assuming no wind) to Biggin Hill only requires the following simple action :—

1. Switch on the Nav receiver. In fact this usually comes on with the communications set.

2. Tune it to 117.5 MHz.

3. Identify the station. Most modern sets have a separate volume control. Turn this up until the airfield information can be heard. Sometimes the knob must be pulled out before the station identification can be heard. Usually the word IDENT is marked on the volume control. When you are satisfied that you are tuned in to a beacon coding 'BIG' the volume may be turned down again.

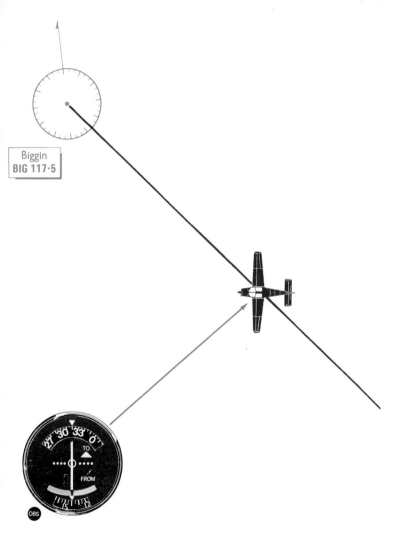

Fig. 4. VOR indicator confirming that the aircraft is on a QDM of 320° TO Biggin. Note that this reading is unaffected by the aircraft's heading at the time.

Biggin
BIG 117·5

4. Using the OBS knob find the QDM to Biggin Hill. You do this by rotating the knob until the LEFT/RIGHT needle is in the centre and the TO/FROM indicator is reading TO. The needle may be centred reading, say, 090° TO or 270° FROM. In other words you may set up the equipment to fly TO a VOR beacon on a particular QDM or FROM the beacon. In this case you want to approach Biggin Hill so the needle must be centred with the indicator reading TO. A word of caution here. The OBS knob requires fine adjustment so when the needle begins to swing towards the centre a gentle touch is needed to place it down the middle.

5. Suppose that the bearing scale reads 320. This means that your QDM to Biggin Hill is 320° and you should turn onto that heading (Fig. 4). While flying towards the VOR beacon the LEFT/RIGHT needle represents your magnetic track. Assuming there is no wind and your flying is very accurate the needle will remain in the centre, running through the little circle. On this day, however, there is a northerly wind and you begin to drift to port. Gradually the needle will swing over to the right and you may interpret this in one of several ways. You could say 'needle right-fly right' or you may regard the instrument as a picture of the situation, your track line moving to the right as you drift to the left. (Fig. 5) In either case you must turn towards the needle to regain track. The point is, by how much should you turn?

6. The dots and the circle are intended to show how far off radial the aircraft is displaced. Full deflection of the needle, left or right, represents 10° when the instrument must be considered inoperative until a new bearing has been found or the aircraft has flown back within 10° of the required

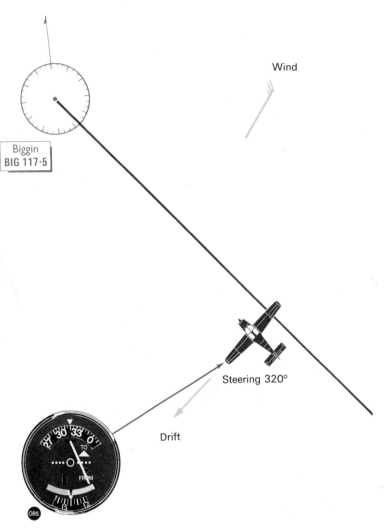

Wind

Biggin
BIG 117·5

Steering 320°

Drift

Fig. 5. Port drift away from QDM 320° causing the VOR indicator to show 'FLY RIGHT'.

11

radial or bearing. When the instrument has four dots marked either side of the circle each dot and the edge of the circle represents 2°. So if the needle has moved over to the first dot on the right you are 4° off track 320°(M) and a correction of 8 to 10° starboard should be tried. If this does the trick the needle will begin to slide towards the centre. If it stays where it is your 8-10° correction is only sufficient to maintain track and you should turn another 10° to starboard in an effort to regain track. When the needle is back in the centre the starboard correction should be halved, otherwise the needle will go to the left indicating a displacement of the aircraft to the right of Track.

7. By now your D.I. may be showing 330° while the VOR indicator is settled on Track 320°, thus confirming that the northerly wind is giving 10° port drift (Fig. 6).

As you approach the VOR beacon its QDMs converge from all points of the compass and in consequence the system becomes more and more sensitive. In fact as the aircraft flies close to the beacon it is almost impossible to control the needle over the last few hundred metres or so. Then it is best to disregard it and concentrate on the DI which has brought you to the beacon on the chosen heading. When the beacon is overflown the needle will move over to one side and a remarkable thing happens — the little indicator flag changes from TO to FROM. And you know you are overhead the beacon. Indeed this is the only time your position is known with certainty when using a single VOR. Why? Because until the indicator changes to FROM the aircraft can be anywhere along the chosen radial — unless of course you have been doing your sums, timing yourself from a previously known position. But remember,

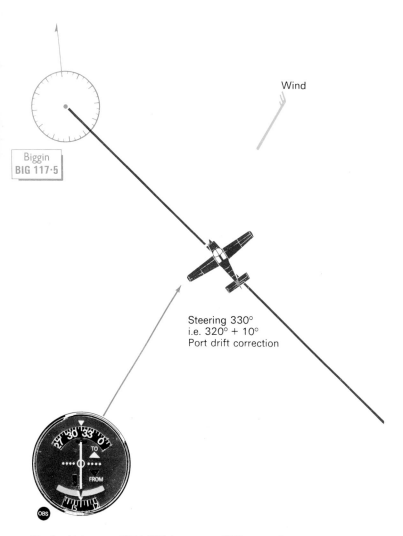

Wind

Biggin
BIG 117·5

Steering 330°
i.e. 320° + 10°
Port drift correction

Fig. 6. Maintaining QDM 320° by steering 330° on the Direction Indicator.
You do **not** steer on the VOR.

13

in the case under discussion you were lost. Now after a few simple actions the aircraft is over Biggin and lunch is only minutes away.

FINDING A POSITION

VOR may be used for 'going' as well as 'coming'. Suppose you wish to fly over a particular area. It could be an airfield without radio aids of any kind or even a town or a lake. You might be required to advise ATC when you are over a reporting point that is not served by its own radio beacon. With a single VOR set you can find the area like this:—

1. Study the radio navigation chart and pick two VOR beacons conveniently placed in relation to the area that has to be overflown. You will need one VOR beacon to guide you towards the area and another that will provide a good 'cut', as near as possible at 90° to track.

2. Note the frequencies and call signs of the two VOR beacons, then measure the magnetic track from the guiding VOR to your area. Next measure the magnetic track from the second VOR, the one that is going to provide a 'cut' and tell you when the area is below the aircraft (or the aircraft is overhead, whichever you prefer).

3. Remember that the LEFT/RIGHT needle ceases to give indications when the aircraft is more than 10° off the selected radial so the plan will be to remain on the first VOR until you are within 10° of the QDM being received from the second VOR beacon. It is a good idea to draw in a 10° line before the 'cut' and measure the distance to where it crosses your track. In this way you will be able to time when to change frequency and set up the second VOR and

so remain on the one guiding you towards the area until the last moment. Although you should have established the correct heading to steer on your DI by that time, it is good practice to remain on the guiding radial as long as possible because there are local wind changes, particularly when flying from coast to inland and the other way round.

4. Make out a simple flight plan. In the air tune the first VOR, identify the call sign, select the required radial then set heading. When you are overhead the departure point note the time and write down the estimated time to within 10° of your 'cut'.

5. Settle on the required radial and check that the indicator is reading FROM. If not you have either set a reciprocal radial on the OBS or you are going the wrong way!

6. It makes life a lot easier if you can find the correct heading to steer on your DI. Remember you cannot fly a heading on the VOR needle — it is only there to show you where magnetic track lies in relation to the aircraft.

7. Watch the time and when you estimate over the 10° mark, change frequency to the second VOR beacon, identify the call sign and set the OBS scale to the bearing TO it from your area, i.e. the 'cut' QDM. WHILE THIS IS GOING ON YOU MUST, REPEAT MUST, MAINTAIN YOUR ORIGINAL HEADING ON THE DI.

8. You are already steering the correct heading towards the required area. All that remains is for you to watch the needle (now representing your 'cut') slide towards the little circle and when it is bang down the middle — you are there (Fig. 7).

Throughout this explanation we have referred to 'the area'. Why not the point or position you may ask. And the

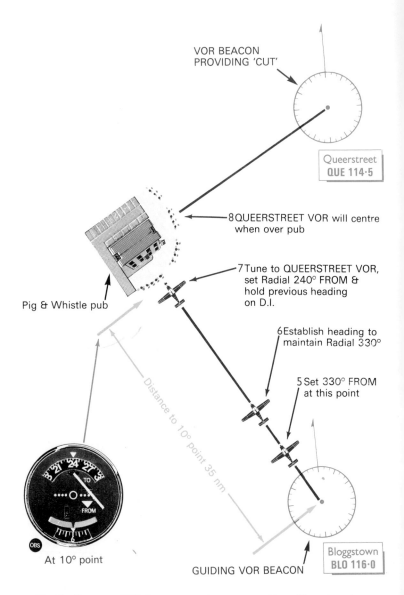

VOR BEACON
PROVIDING 'CUT'

Queerstreet
QUE 114·5

8 QUEERSTREET VOR will centre
when over pub

7 Tune to QUEERSTREET VOR,
set Radial 240° FROM &
hold previous heading
on D.I.

Pig & Whistle pub

6 Establish heading to
maintain Radial 330°

5 Set 330° FROM
at this point

Distance to 10° point 35 nm

OBS

At 10° point

GUIDING VOR BEACON

Bloggstown
BLO 116·0

Fig. 7. Using two VOR Beacons to arrive over a position. The red numbers
5, 6, 7 & 8 relate to the text on page 15.

16

answer is that in this world nothing is perfect, not even VOR. The equipment is not 100% accurate and such errors as exist magnify as you fly away from the beacon. There will be more about these errors later but at this stage you should content yourself with the knowledge that at worst VOR will get you to 'the area' if not within a few yards. At best i.e. when flying to overhead the beacon it is VERY accurate. And there are plenty of convenient VOR beacons throughout Europe and of course North America.

The exercise just described, finding an area by using two VOR beacons was conducted on an aircraft fitted with a single Nav receiver and a single Omni-bearing Indicator. Most commercial and indeed many light aircraft carry two sets. Think how easy it is then. Or if your aircraft has ADF as well as a VOR set very often a conveniently placed NDB may be used to provide a 'cut' at the required area.

Suppose you wish to approach the beacon on a particular heading. You may have to do this for the purpose of avoiding a danger area or controlled airspace. Or the visibility could be bad and you want to arrive in line with the runway in use. We call this

INTERCEPTING A REQUIRED RADIAL.

Let us be clear about terms. Radials are FROM the beacon and since the VOR transmitter is always set up relative to Magnetic North it follows that the radial is in fact a magnetic track AWAY from the beacon. In the previous exercise we flew along a radial to the required area and although the beacon was behind us the LEFT/RIGHT needle continued to give corrective information in the natural sense because the indicator flag was reading

FROM. Had we in error set up the OBS on a 180° reciprocal the needle would have centred as before but this time with the flag indicating TO. Then the LEFT/RIGHT needle would tell you to fly left when it should be right and right when it should be left. Which is your fault entirely because with the flag showing TO you are supposed to be going the other way. It is simply a matter of the pub being on your right when facing up the High Street and on your left when you do an about turn. So to re-cap: while bearings or tracks may be TO or FROM, VOR RADIALS are always FROM the beacon.

How do you intercept one? It goes like this:—

1. You are somewhere to the East of Southend, over the water, rather conscious of their Special Rules Zone and all those car ferries flying in and out. You are making for Biggin Hill and in order to avoid the Southend Zone a decision is made to approach the destination on Radial 100 which will keep you clear of the SRZ boundary. A glance at the Radio Nav Chart shows that Radial 090 runs close to the edge of the Southend SRZ so no attempt should be made to head out west until you have passed that magnetic bearing FROM Biggin Hill (Fig. 8).

2. How far east of Southend are you? This is important. Avoiding the Zone by flying along Radial 100 is one thing. Clobbering the Zone on the way to the radial is another and very real possibility. Fortunately there are other friendly VOR beacons in the area and it is a few seconds task to tune in to one in this case north or south of your estimated position; Clacton VOR would be ideal. Uncertain of position you may be but it is at least on the cards that the beacon is somewhere to the north and therefore ideally

18

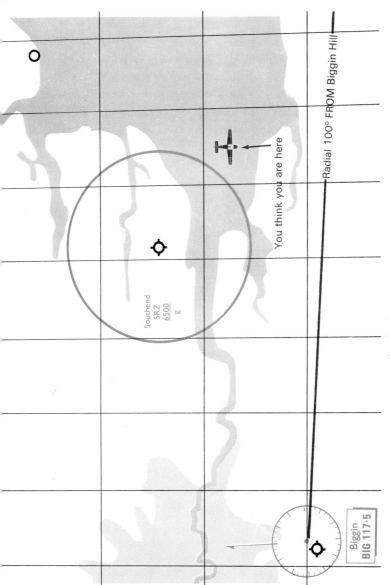

Southend
SRZ
6500
g

You think you are here

Radial 100° FROM Biggin Hill

Biggin
BIG 117·5

Fig. 8. Lost over the Sea!

19

positioned to hold you clear of the eastern edge of the Southend SRZ. So tune in to 115.7, identify the callsign CLN (—·—· ·—·· —·) then turn the OBS until the LEFT/RIGHT needle centres with the flag reading FROM. And there it is, your radial from Clacton reading 195 (Fig. 9).

3. A look at the London Area Chart will confirm that if the aircraft continues to follow Clacton Radial 195 it will pass well to the east of the Southend SRZ, so maintain this radial by finding the heading to steer on your DI. A few minutes watching the needle will confirm if there is any drift and you can adjust your heading (on the DI) as necessary to keep the VOR needle centred. Now tune in to the Biggin Hill VOR, identify the callsign then turn the OBS until the LEFT/RIGHT needle centres with the flag reading FROM. The azimuth scale reads 075 and you can see from the chart that this radial from Biggin Hill will take you through the Southend SRZ, in fact not far south of the airfield. There is a long way to go before reaching Radial 100 and it may be a good idea to go back to the Clacton VOR for another five minutes just to check that the wind is not drifting you in towards the zone (Fig. 10).

4. Tune in the Biggin VOR again and using the previously explained method, find the radial to the beacon. Probably by now you will have reached Radial 090 or thereabouts. In any case you are well clear of the SRZ so why not cut the corner a little? This will save a few minutes flying time and enable you to close with Radial 100 at a smaller angle (Fig. 11). So far we have been dealing in Radials, or Magnetic Bearings from the beacons. This is convenient because when using Radio Navigation Charts the compass rose shown around VOR beacons gives information FROM.

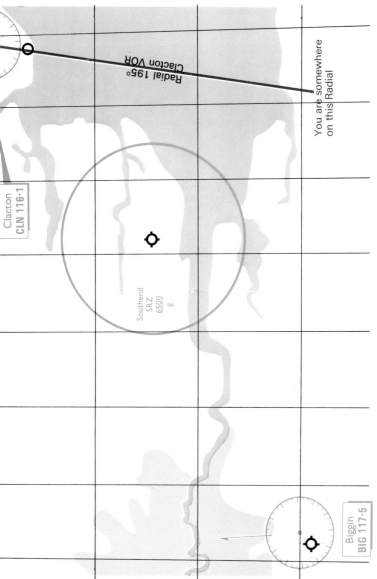

Clacton
CLN 116·1

Clacton VOR
Radial 195°

You are somewhere
on this Radial

Southend
SRZ
6500
g

Biggin
BIG 117·5

Fig. 9. Using Clacton VOR to keep out of the Southend Special Rules Zone.

21

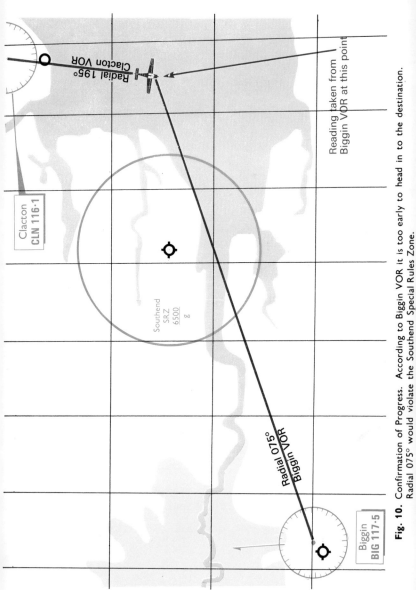

Fig. 10. Confirmation of Progress. According to Biggin VOR it is too early to head in to the destination. Radial 075° would violate the Southend Special Rules Zone.

Reading taken from Biggin VOR at this point

Clacton VOR

Radial 195° Clacton VOR

Clacton
CLN 116·1

Southend
SRZ
6500
g

Radial 075°
Biggin VOR

Biggin
BIG 117·5

22

Fig. 11. While Radial 090° is clear of the Southend Zone Radial 100° is safer. At this point the corner could be cut, saving time and easing accurate interception of the required Radial.

23

However, now you are going to track in towards Biggin Hill and the LEFT/RIGHT needle must be made to provide information in the natural sense. Remember it can only do this when the flag agrees that you are flying TO or FROM the beacon. So although it is intended to fly along Radial 100, you must fly along a QDM of 280° (M) to reach the beacon, i.e. the reciprocal of the radial. If you dislike doing sums in the air they have thoughtfully added a reciprocal scale opposite the main setting but now you are closing with the radial and you must set 280 TO on the VOR indicator.

5. Having set 280 TO on the OBS the rest is so easy. Just watch the LEFT/RIGHT needle. It will be showing a full 'FLY LEFT' command at this stage but as you close with the radial, approaching it from the right, the needle will start to come in towards the centre. Remember that each dot represents approximately 2° track error and the nearer you are to the station the more closely spaced are the radials. Think of the spokes of a bicycle wheel. You are still some distance from Biggin Hill because the chosen radial has been intercepted on a southerly heading to the East of Southend so it would be as well to start a gradual turn towards 280 TO when the needle shows you to be within two degrees or so of that QDM. Had you been closer to the VOR beacon the turn would have started 5° or even 10° before reaching the QDM. Remember that bicycle wheel again and you will readily see why this is so (Fig. 12).

6. By now the aircraft is tracking in towards the beacon and a heading to steer must be found. You must have some idea of the wind and a little thought will produce some approximation of the likely drift Port or Starboard of 280°

24

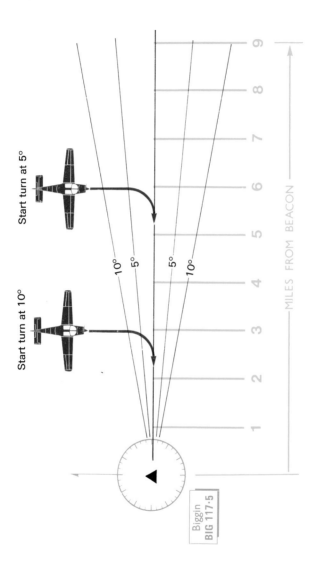

Fig. 12. The closer the Beacon, the earlier the turn.

Start turn at 5°

Start turn at 10°

10°

5°

5°

10°

MILES FROM BEACON

Biggin
BIG 117·5

Magnetic. You may wish to be thoroughly lazy and do without the sums. In this case, just fly 280° for a few moments (having checked your DI with the Magnetic Compass) and see what happens. A FLY RIGHT command means you have port drift and a little trial and error will place the aircraft back in business with the LEFT/RIGHT needle in the centre and an appropriate new heading on the DI. Remember to steer on the DI. You cannot do this on the VOR indicator. It is only there to tell you where the aircraft is in relation to the beacon and your chosen track or radial.

7. How are we progressing? How close are we to Biggin Hill? Even with a single NAV set we can find out by enlisting the help of another VOR beacon situated to the left or right of track. There is a convenient one for the case under discussion at Seaford on the south coast only there is a snag here. VOR being a VHF aid is entirely dependent upon 'line of sight' for reception (high and medium frequencies have a ground and a reflected wave which bounces back from the reflective areas in the upper air) and there is some high ground between the coast and the Biggin Hill area. Unless you are flying at over 2000 feet it is unlikely you will receive Seaford which is a pity because it is ideal for the purpose of obtaining a 'cut' on Biggin Hill (Fig. 13). In fact Biggin Hill lies pretty well on 360 FROM Seaford. Assuming you can receive Seaford it is vital that a steady heading is maintained while tuning to the new beacon and checking the radial. There would be little point in finding your approximate distance to the beacon at the expense of keeping track.

8. Of course it is so much easier to make a distance check

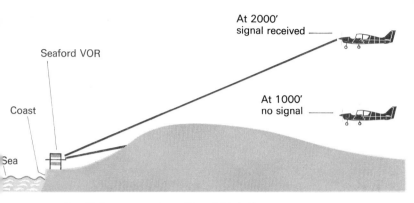

Fig. 13. Lost contact due to 'line-of-sight' effect.

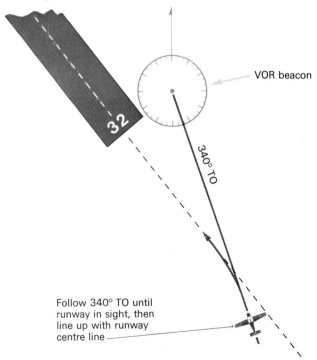

Fig. 14. Using a convenient VOR Beacon to find the runway.

when there are two VOR sets. You simply line up one set on Biggin Hill for guidance to the airfield while the other NAV receiver is tuned to Seaford, its OBS being adjusted from time to time to keep the needle centred and so give some idea of progress. This is all we require. However a single VOR set will tell you when the beacon is below the aircraft — the LEFT/RIGHT needle swings over and the flag goes from TO to FROM. There is another piece of radio magic available for the purpose of giving distance TO or FROM a beacon. DME or Distance Measuring Equipment. This will be described later.

THE VOR LET-DOWN

Any let-down through cloud, whatever the radio aid used for the purpose, demands a satisfactory degree of instrument flying skill. You can have two of everything in the aircraft but without proficiency in the basic technique of instrument flying the radio might as well be left switched off for all the good it will do unless of course you are flying in VMC. The purpose of any let-down procedure is to bring the aircraft through cloud so that risk of collision with high obstacles or other traffic is avoided and a safe landing can be effected. Its other purpose is to position the aircraft for a landing when the visibility prevents a line-up with the landing area using the 'eyeball method'. Let-down charts are available for all airfields having an approved procedure and when more than one radio aid is available, a separate chart is produced for each aid. You are entitled to ask why. The point is that some radio aids are more precise than others. And clearly the more accurate the aid, the lower the limit to which you may descend during an instrument approach. As a matter of interest, Radar and Instrument Landing System are very accurate radio landing aids; VDF and ADF are less so, in fact really only regarded as let down through cloud (**cloud break**) aids. VOR falls somewhere between the best and the worst but although a beacon situated on an airfield is usually sited to one side of the runway, good results may be obtained by planning to approach at a slight angle to the centre line QDM (Fig. 14). Let-down charts offer a lot of vital information; high ground, minimum safe altitudes within the area covered, available radio aids and their frequencies and two diagrams of the let-down and overshoot procedure, one in elevation and the other in plan. They also quote the OCL (obstacle clearance limit). This is the lowest safe level to which you may descend on that particular aid. It is usual practice to increase the OCL figure on the chart up to the nearest 50 feet, then add another 50 for the wife and kids. These very general notes are not intended to teach you how to do a VOR approach in vile weather. If you have ambitions to achieve the required standards the subject is handled in more detail and depth in FLIGHT BRIEFING FOR PILOTS, VOLUME 3. Sufficient to say that VOR may be used as a break cloud aid, or in expert hands as an approach aid. Its use is further enhanced during bad weather landing because your NAV set may be tuned to the Instrument Landing System if there is one at the airfield. Then the OBS becomes inoperative and the LEFT/RIGHT needle represents the runway centre line. Full deflection relates to approximately $2\frac{1}{2}°$ off runway centre so in the ILS mode your VOR indicator is very accurate indeed. Do bear in mind that when you elect to use your VOR for an ILS approach it provides only one third of the story. Full ILS has another needle to indicate glide path and a marker receiver to tell the pilot when he is over the Outer and Middle Markers. Even so the needle you have will respond to the ILS Localizer and this in itself is a great help. Most VOR indicators do in fact have a blue and a yellow quadrant marked left and right of centre. These two markings relate to the blue and yellow sectors shown left and right of the runway on ILS charts (Fig. 15).

LIMITATIONS OF VOR

Having said so many nice things about VOR, its simplicity, light weight and relative cheapness, the reader must by now be asking himself 'what are the snags — nothing can be so good'. There is, of course, a snag and a hint was dropped on page 17. It is this. Due to slight inaccuracies at the transmitter, the bending effect of the ground with its varying electric conductivity, the bending effects of the aircraft receiving the signal, inaccuracies in the receiver and the instrument itself a good VOR reading cannot be more accurate than plus or minus 3° while a poor one might be as much as five or even six degrees out. If you think back to your PPL exams and the bit about pilot navigation, somewhere in the dark will be lurking fond memories of the 'one-in-sixty' rule. You will recall that some bright chap discovered how one unit left or right of a line sixty of the same units long represented one degree angle. So if the aircraft is 60 miles from the beacon flying on the VOR, at best you can only expect to be within three miles of where the needle says you are and it could be six miles left or right of required track. And at a distance of 120 miles the error will double. However the situation is not quite so bad

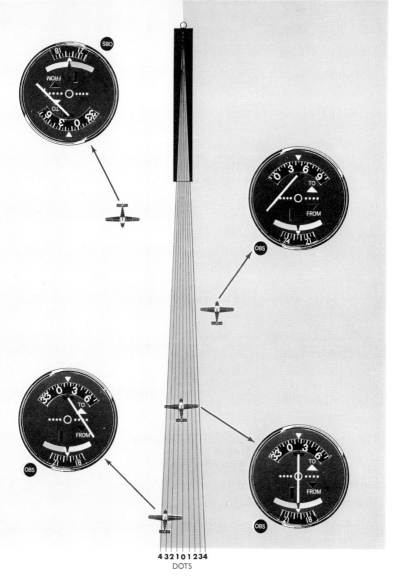

4 3 2 1 0 1 2 3 4
DOTS

Fig. 15. Using the VOR indicator for an ILS approach. When an ILS frequency is selected the TO/FROM indicator remains at TO, the OBS becomes inactive and each dot represents approximately ½° from runway centre. Note that although when flying a reciprocal to the ILS heading 'Fly Left/Fly Right' signals are reversed, the needle always indicates the correct side of the runway (blue or yellow), e.g. the top left instrument.

31

as it seems. There are a lot of beacons throughout Europe and other parts of the world so there is rarely any need to use VOR at the limit of its useful range. Indeed it was never intended to be a long range aid. Then again the most common procedure with VOR is flying TO the beacon. Then the aid becomes more and more accurate as you near the transmitter which is fine because in many cases you are aiming to be where these beacons are situated anyway.

So often the history of modern invention has been that Britain was the innovator then some other country, usually the USA went ahead and developed the idea to the point of mass production. VOR is rather different in that the Americans were the innovators and now a British company has evolved a new development working on the doppler principle. You need know nothing of how this operates but the main factor of pilot interest is that it is more accurate than existing VOR beacons, to a large extent eliminating those radial bends caused by ground effect.

VOR DEVELOPMENTS IN COMMON USE
The newer doppler VOR beacons will improve accuracy as they come into operation but what of the aircraft equipment, those little black boxes (why do they always seem to be black?) which are under the control of the pilot. Here are some of the improved VOR sets in common use.

PICTORIAL DISPLAYS
As the term implies, these indicators are arranged to present information in a manner more representative of reality than the standard omni-bearing indicator. There are a number of these units made by the leading electronics firms and usually the LEFT/RIGHT needle is attached to a

backplate arranged to rotate with the aircraft's heading. In fact it is often fed by the gyro-compass. If you think about it this is quite a breakthrough because now the needle will provide a true picture of track, not only when flying to or from the beacon but also on those occasions when the radial has to be intercepted at an angle of up to 90°. The illusion of flying towards the track line is made the more real by a little aeroplane etched in plan form on the glass of the instrument. There is the usual OBS knob but instead of rotating a compass card as it does on the simple omni-bearing indicator the entire needle and dot system is aligned with the compass ring. A separate knob moves a little index (called a **bug**) which indicates the heading to be steered. The usual TO/FROM indicator is replaced by an arrowhead which always points to the beacon.

Most of these instruments have built in ILS glideslope indicators and when the set is tuned to an ILS frequency the glideslope facility comes into play (Fig. 16).

AREA NAVIGATION (RNAV)

One of the limitations of any aid related to bearings from a fixed point is that, for practical purposes, all air traffic is confined to 'beacon bashing' i.e. tiptoeing from beacon to beacon like a man crossing a river on stepping stones. Added to this pilots are entitled to expect training on radio aids and in consequence some of the more popular beacons attract club aircraft like flies around the unmentionable and this turns the peaceful air into Indian Country where airline pilots fear to venture.

True area navigation is expensive, the Decca system being an outstanding example of accurate, convenient equipment

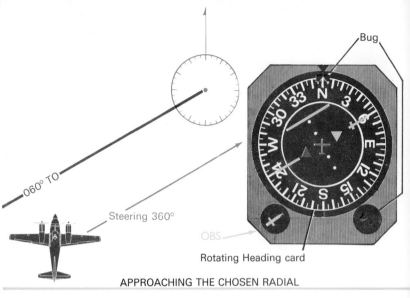

APPROACHING THE CHOSEN RADIAL

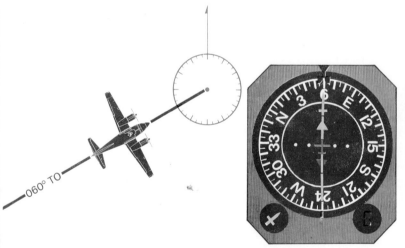

ON THE CHOSEN RADIAL

Fig. 16. Combined Gyro Compass and VOR Indicator which presents the VOR Radial in the correct position relative to the aircraft. Required Heading is set on the right-hand knob and indicated by the 'bug'. Required VOR Radial is selected on the left-hand knob. These simple to use instruments are sometimes called Horizontal Situation Indicators.

that is quite out of the financial reach of most small aircraft operators. An extension of VOR which gives area nav. capabilities is however available. It works this way. Suppose you want to break cloud over an airfield without radio nav. or landing aids. You find the nearest VOR beacon, measure its bearing and distance to your destination and set this on the RNAV computer which will then offset the VOR beacon so that it appears to be sited on your airfield, lake, cricket pitch or whatever is your pleasure. The 'ghost' VOR may be used as though it existed when in fact the actual beacon is some miles away.

While the aid is of great value in so far as it is capable of relieving traffic congestion by providing an infinite number of 'ghost' VOR beacons or **waypoints**, RNAV is nevertheless a 'poor man's substitute for the real thing because along with the beacon are moved all the usual errors of the system. It is pretty good even so.

DISTANCE MEASURING EQUIPMENT (DME)

Although DME is nothing like VOR in principle it is often used in conjunction with the omni-bearing indicator and indeed DME transmitters are sited with VOR beacons so that bearing and distance information may be provided. For convenience DME frequencies are paired with their related VOR frequency. You select frequency on the DME receiver in the usual way and within a few seconds a reading will come up. It may be presented as an enlarged version of the familiar car mileometer or there can be a pointer sweeping over a scale calibrated in miles. When flying to or from the beacon DME will also provide a groundspeed so it is quite a box of tricks. The value of DME is that used in conjunction with VOR you have a very complete picture of location in relation to the beacon thus eliminating the need to re-tune and obtain a 'cut' with another VOR beacon. A word of warning here. Not all VOR beacons have DME facility so if you have a DME set in your aircraft do not be surprised if the numbers spin round and around when you tune to a non-starter.

LETS HAVE A RECAP

One could go on and on about VOR or for that matter any radio aid. But this little book is only intended to introduce VOR to the newcomer and there is enough in the foregoing pages to make him feel at home with his new toy. In conclusion here is a summary of facts about VOR.

VOR is a short-range radio navigation aid operating on VHF.

VOR is received on the NAV part of your NAV/COM set.

VOR operates within a separate range of frequencies to those used for communications.

VOR is known as a Phase Comparison aid.

VOR will provide Radials FROM or QDMs TO the station.

VOR bearings are always related to Magnetic North.

VOR transmissions include the beacon call sign in morse and sometimes a continuous ATIS* broadcast.

VOR has a bearing accuracy of between 3° and 6° left or right of track.

VOR will only give a position when the beacon is overflown.

Then the LEFT/RIGHT needle will swing over and the flag will change from TO to FROM (assuming it was set to TO when flying to the beacon).

VOR will only provide corrective needle indications when it is set to read TO while flying to the beacon or FROM when tracking away from the beacon.

VOR information is displayed on an Omni-Bearing Indicator.

*Automatic Terminal Information Service.

VOR radials FROM or magnetic bearings TO the beacon are selected on the Omni-Bearing selector (OBS).

This rotates a compass card which also provides the reciprocal in smaller figures.

VOR may be used in conjunction with other aids and two VOR sets will provide continuous position information by using the other set to obtain a suitable 'cut' along the track being flown.

VOR may be used with pictorial displays which present the chosen radial or QDM in its true relationship with the aircraft.

VOR may be used in conjunction with DME to provide a constant bearing and distance from the Beacon.

VOR may be fed into a computer designed to provide offset facility. This enables the pilot to select waypoints, i.e. to move existing VOR beacons to any position within the range of the equipment. Then it is called RNAV.

VOR transmitter accuracy has been improved in new equipment using the doppler principle.

VOR instruments will indicate up to 10° left or right of the chosen setting. When the aircraft strays very far from the chosen setting the 'OFF' flag will appear, warning that the instrument cannot indicate the true picture until it is re-set to within 10° of its magnetic bearing in relation to the beacon.

THINGS TO DO

DO check that you have the correct VOR frequency for your chosen beacon.

DO check the callsign before pressing on into the murk.

DO select the bearing scale with care. Remember one little degree at a distance of 60 miles will add a full mile to the existing errors.

DO keep on your toes when nearing the beacon. The QDMs are converging here and the aid is becoming increasingly accurate. If you are to pass overhead the beacon you too will have to fly accurately.

DO set the OBS so that the instrument reads TO when flying to the beacon and FROM while flying away, that is if you want it to correct in the proper sense.

DO remember to re-set your DI with the magnetic compass, for preference every fifteen minutes or so.

DO allow for the radius of turn when joining a radial or QDM at an angle of more than 30°. Remember the spokes of that cycle wheel converging to the centre and you will then allow more deflection on the needle when starting a turn near the beacon than when you are, say, thirty or so miles away.

DO NOTS

DO NOT attempt to steer on the VOR indicator. It is there to tell you where the beacon is and where you are in relation to the chosen magnetic track. You must steer on the DI.

DO NOT try to use the indicator reading FROM when you are inbound the beacon or reading TO when flying outbound. It will give reversed commands and get you good and truly lost.

DO NOT attempt to let down into hilly country on the basis of VOR readings obtained some distance away from the beacon. The aid is not accurate enough under these circumstances. Save your VOR let-downs for the beacon end of the flight.

DO NOT continue using the VOR indicator after it has assumed full deflection left or right. The Omni-bearing Indicator is then out of business and you must find another bearing or fly back within the existing setting without delay.

DO NOT use the VOR at long range. Try and find a nearer beacon and if there is nothing available use the best other aid at your disposal. 100 miles is a good maximum range for everyday use.

And finally if one day you are flying along with the needle bang in the middle, mile after mile, minute after minute, do check that the 'OFF' flag has not appeared. If it has the needle will indeed be in the middle but not because of your impeccable flying. Either the set has packed up or the VOR beacon has gone off the air. Turn up the volume control and if nothing is coming through, try another frequency. If that is dead also your set has packed up for the day. Alternatively when other stations are receivable most likely this means that your favourite VOR is off the air. And we all need a holiday sometimes!

IDENTIFYING THE CALL SIGN

LETTERS

A	Alpha	• —	N	November	— •
B	Bravo	— • • •	O	Oscar	— — —
C	Charlie	— • — •	P	Papa	• — — •
D	Delta	— • •	Q	Quebec	— — • —
E	Echo	•	R	Romeo	• — •
F	Foxtrot	• • — •	S	Sierra	• • •
G	Golf	— — •	T	Tango	—
H	Hotel	• • • •	U	Uniform	• • —
I	India	• •	V	Victor	• • • —
J	Juliett	• — — —	W	Whiskey	• — —
K	Kilo	— • —	X	X-ray	— • • —
L	Lima	• — • •	Y	Yankee	— • — —
M	Mike	— —	Z	Zulu	— — • •

FIGURES

1	• — — — —	6	— • • • •
2	• • — — —	7	— — • • •
3	• • • — —	8	— — — • •
4	• • • • —	9	— — — — •
5	• • • • •	0	— — — — —